300/4D

The Phoenix Living Poets

★

UNLAWFUL ASSEMBLY

by

D. J. Enright

CHATTO AND WINDUS

THE HOGARTH PRESS

1968

Published by
Chatto and Windus Ltd
with The Hogarth Press Ltd
42 William IV Street
London WC2
*
Clarke, Irwin and Co Ltd
Toronto

Acknowledgements are due to the editors of the
following periodicals, in which some of the poems
in this book originally appeared: *Encounter, The
Hudson Review, The Listener, The London Magazine,
The Malahat Review, Meanjin Quarterly, New
Statesman, Observer, Poetry Book Society Bulletin, The
Sunday Times, The Times Literary Supplement,
Transition* (Uganda).

SBN 7011 1367 7

Printed in Great Britain by
William Lewis (Printers) Limited
Cardiff

Contents

The Accents of Brecht

The sour breath of the underfed
Stood in the overloaded roads.
The farmers sold their daughters,
Daughters sold their flesh and blood.

In that country one almost came
To emulate the accents of Brecht.
Plain speaking was in order,
Plain speaking was merely truth.

These days things are looking up,
One sees more cars on better streets,
Although no revolution intervenes,
No heroes. Nothing much to write about.

Simply: 'One another we must love or
Show no profits,' they explained.
If this put paid to the accents of Brecht,
Who am I then to complain?

The Small War

Our teachers taught us to distrust,
Taught toads to squat upon our chest.
We know that every broken beggar
On the streets was once a chooser:

That casualties are not that high,
And bombs dropped by a near-ally
Are well intentioned if not aimed:
That peasants cannot but be lamed

In agile wars of ideology:
That protest is perversity,
And no one's so unpleasing as a saint
Forever strumming his long-haired complaint.

The good life is no special gain
Unless defined by loss and pain.
For some still pay the price for others,
In songs alone are all men brothers.

We saw our simple parents suffer.
A richer diet has made us tougher,
And since man's enemy cannot be fought,
We fight the men he might defeat.

Our teachers taught us to distrust,
Taught toads to squat upon our chest.
Their swollen bellies and their tiny roars
Mock foreign bones on alien shores.

The rebels grow weary.
And no wonder! —
Suns still shine, rains fall,
And all the same
A stadium
Is enjoyed by many.
Rice and basketball,
Papayas plumping goldenly,
The beggar has her baby.
Nature sponsors all,
In some degree.

But to spend a life in gaol! —
That stable climate.
Better the State's polluted breath
Than your own small bag of stale
Breathed in and out and in and out.
We die, and the rice will eat us —
But not for politics,
It seems, not death,
Not any longer.

For the State lives for ever,
And
(Easily caught, this habit)
Once a prisoner, always a prisoner.
To die for one's own belief —
What is it, but murder
By one's child?

So,
Petitions are submitted
(Better to lose face
Than family),
Guarantees are given.
'I will be good.'
'I will be seen but not heard.'
'I will cultivate my garden.'
(Odd, that papayas grow so happily
In this polluted air —
Like moss in prison!)

The rebels grow weary.
Tools of Moscow,
Valets des valets
Des impérialistes américains,
Or agents of Peking,
Running dogs or sheep astray —
Man does not live by faith alone.
The gods are failing,
Faster every day,
Their temples emptying.

It's an Art

Poets are not concerned
With the streaks on the tulip,
The small red appearances.

And the art of poetry is
Not to say everything.
Much virtue in obliquity!

If you know already, you can tell
From this massive obliquity
That one lives in a time of war.

The war being oblique.
Which is to say:
Elsewhere.

That one knows at all
Is the doing of a rabble of
Newspapermen.

Venal scribblers of
Purple passages and
Red-streaked reportage.

Oblique! —
Vietnam has neither made nor marred a poet.
The art of poetry is not to say a thing.

'What is poet?'
Asks the little girl in school.
'A rare sort of bird,'

Says teacher,
'Still heard occasionally on a quiet night.
The BBC has tape recordings.'

Roman Reasons

No wide-eyed innocent, he
Had heard tell of villainy,
Had noticed
That one's loot was one's pay.
Yet he could say
— Seeking no comfort in numbers,
In mutuality's immunity —
'I am alone the villain of the earth.'

Finding good reasons
(Reasons are good),
Finding reasons
For the serial assassinations,
For the quotidian killings
(One's pay was one's loot),
The convenient weddings,
And the other treasons.
But not for what he had done.

Despite the logic, the prior logic,
The good, the worthy reasons,
Ratified by that old manual
He carried in his head,
Those *Hints for Roman Soldiers,*
Those counsels scratched in red —

The reasons, the decent reasons,
Each day stronger,
For his leaving their service
— An ageing general, all heart and no brain,

An ageing native woman, wrinkles and wiles —
Who couldn't be served any longer.

And yet, when it was done,
Expeditiously and quietly done —
An emperor, a Jove, a breaker of hearts,
A queen, a Venus, a breaker of hearts.
Larger than life — unfair, unfair!
From time to time men die, it would seem,
For love, and the crocodiles eat them.

Healthy, cheerful, realistic. Yet
Somehow unable to excuse himself,
Those *Hints* less lucid than he'd thought,
And logic a botched breastplate.
Alone the villain of the earth. Alone.
So, heart failure in a ditch.
Expeditiously and quietly done,
Unnoticed by *Les Nouvelles d'Egypte*
Or the Roman *Gazette,*
Their columns packed with acts and scenes —

Enobarbus, wine-bearded captain,
You are the hero of my play!

They dart or lurch, collide or embrace
(Beaks long, for what? Eyes red, with what?)
They chirp, they screech, they whistle.

Whether the starlings are
Making love or making war
— That I cannot tell.

They meet or they part,
They give or they take,
They jostle or nestle.

I cannot be sure
— So many of them, so many! —
I know what I like to think.

They are full of life
(One's eyes blur with grateful water)
They are living, lively, full of life.

Off duty too,
Ten twilight minutes for indulgence,
Hand cupped beneath the chin,

Some grander watcher,
Watching us (with maybe grateful, maybe blurring eyes),
Will he know what he likes to think?

They are full of life
— So many of them, so many! —
They are so lively, living, full of life.

Writing Poetry in a Hotel Room

Is it to tame the place perhaps
— though heaven knows it's hardly
wild? To beautify the spot
— it's not exactly ugly?

To clear a space where one can walk
    on homely naked feet?
Or make room in the room
    for possibilities of sleep?

Not home (the waiting word) since
    home is where you left it.
Why organise one here, and
    waste the airline ticket?

Away's away. It's simply, if
    the bedside rug is grubby,
Kick it underneath the bed.
    Compound with that nude lady

who bears a faded lampshade
    on her brassy head. Learn
the quiddities of cupboards,
    where curtains draw the line.

Till the paperbasket's wastes
    and harvest the *belle vue*.
To open neutral ground
    is one thing poetry can do —

and grow on it: as one might
    even say, a sort of culture. All
the laws of science couldn't white-
    wash that nude lady of the deadly shade;

nor measurement of stress and strain
    lay me soundly down to sleep
in this typhonic wind and rain.
    I'll rather write of sampans

overturning. No, there's no need to —
    I've formed relations with this room,
cool but adequate. I don't mean
    to marry it, and take it home.

Come to Sunny S

You step down over the silvery sea,
Under the blue air, and there you find
The roads are rather Roman, and Guinness
Is served ice-cold in the wine-shops,
That the buildings are modern, or else
Middle-aged, no older than you are.

The British have left GO-CAUTION-STOP
At intersections. Park opposite a
White line, you will surely be fined.
No mystery, simply a white line, a fine.
The laws are rather Roman too.

There are no nautch-girls here,
No geisha, no sing-song girls, indeed
We have nothing along those lines except
Girls.

Our temples were erected yesterday,
And renovated this morning. We see no
Virtue in decay. Our schools face the old
Problem: children. Our scent is chiefly
Petrol. Our shops sell what we need.

Among our customs, self-sacrifice to
Tourists is not one. We sell you
What you can get at Harrod's or Liberty's
But, being the East, a little cheaper.

We do not sell virgins cheap,
We need them. If you prick us, we shall
Probably bleed. For a price you can get
What you can get at home for a price.
We are not certain what we are, we are
Various. You will write books later and
Tell us. We shall display your books
In our tourist hotels.

Our speciality is race riots: which
Wouldn't interest you half as much as
The forbidden dances of temple prostitutes
(Tickets sold at all Government offices)
Or the Spring Festival (held every Saturday)
Of a special class of female artist —
Neither of which we have in this country.

Our speciality is human trouble:
Which mightn't appeal to you, seeing
You could get your heads, breasts or
Balls sliced off accidentally. This
Is our only form of human sacrifice.

And I tell you this because I think
You may be human.

A Dry Palm

Fronds are dancing in the wind,
A drawn-out din of movement.
Yet only one of them is heard —

A dead one, all but dead,
Alive by the skin of its sallow foot,
Its carking, carping voice.

A wary veteran, hardly daring
To stir, far less to dance.
But doing all the talking.

Brief Briefing

Colourful? It's green here,
Green and green. And then
A spectrum of ideologies —

Where too much colour
(Discernible red, let's say)
Spells detention.

And too much green
Means jungle here again.
They cut back both.

The spectrum fades to grey,
And grey apartment houses
Elbow out the jungle.

But then the flags of washing
Streaming out from poles —
It's all the colours here!

After the Gods, after the Heroes

You can see how easily a man is silenced.
Merely two or three helpers to twist his arms
Behind his back, shove him into a conveniently
Parked vehicle, drive him to a quiet place and
Beat his teeth in. Eventually he falls silent.

Don't talk about heroism. Its lifetime is a breath.
Heroes with bullets in their heads are just
Bodies. Their families are put to the expense of
Burying them. Even the quietest funeral costs money.

Opinion is informed these days. No one's readily
Excited. There have been so many heroes.
Sensibility alters from generation to generation, and
The general feeling is that people who get into trouble
Are troublesome. And the ones who fail to recover are
Born suicides.

In any case, can even the expert tell a hero from a
Villain? What are the distinguishing marks?

The history books are full already.
You can't buy space in the papers for love or money.
The papers are occupied with quintuplets, with modes,
With civil murder, with the heroism of pet dogs.
Don't adduce the inspirational power of example
But rather the dehortative authority of example.
No use talking of freedom as if it were an essential
Vegetable or a family car. You are talking to
Knowledgeable men and women, who eat vegetables, who
Own cars.

It hurts to say so, but in our time
Perhaps you will have to rely on the others, on
Paterfamilias and materfamilias, clerks bored by their
Desks, graduates with pass degrees and no special field,
Grandads out for a last fling, girls with odd fancies,
Boys who would write verse, if they could, and get it
Off their chests . . .
Those non-heroes that the poorest country's rich in.

The leaders of the masses seem to have stopped
Leading. Now you are left with the masses.
Their separate preferences and small tenacious ambitions,
Their tendency (being too many to shoot or put in prison)
To survive in private.

Either that, or else go hang yourself, and
Die in private. Leave an open letter, dignified,
Reproachful. Also, if the papers are to print it,
Irreproachable and brief.

What became of What-was-his-name?

Roughly once a quarter
I think of M—.
He must have been inside
For about three years now.
And three months longer
Each time I think of him.

Not that I knew him well.
But he used to hang around the place,
Looking for odd scraps of news.
Not a bad newspaperman,
I used to think,
A graduate with some ability
To express himself,
Comparatively well-mannered,
And properly sceptical
About the official hand-outs.
He would ask you what *you* thought.

Others have gone in
And come out
Since then,
Have taken new jobs and
Fathered new babies.
L— and F— are still inside,
But they're hard-core,
Prison is their favourite freedom.
M— wasn't that sort,
He seemed to me a food and drink man.
But he must have done something very bad.
The papers said nothing about it.

One could ask.
But it would draw attention to you,
And to M—.
They say the cases are reviewed
Every twelve months,
And it wouldn't do him any good
For the Special Branch to mention,
'He was asked after by . . .'

Like the police
In that other country:
'What would a gentleman like you
Want with those fellows?'
No use to answer:
'Well, it's only that
I've been teaching them English
For the past two or three years,
And . . .'
No one believes in pure friendship,
Charity went out
When Aid came in.

'Remember, this isn't Oxford or
Cambridge, you know.'
And then they might ask M—:
'Why would a foreigner be
Interested in you?
What favours have you done this
Foreigner?'
M— had better be totally uninteresting.

Is M— married, I wonder?
I can't remember whether I ever knew.
His wife would have news of him,
But she'll have returned to her family,
To her village.
It's not done
To pursue people to their villages.

Funny,
After three years
A new generation hangs around the place,
Hardly one of them has heard of M—.
It makes you feel your age.

But one thing's certain,
M— is alive.
They don't shoot people hereabouts,
They need to review them every year.
M— is a sort of pet, I suppose,
I remember him every three months.
Not that I ever knew him well.

Footsteps

Oh law-abiding country! —
Whose loyal robbers enter
Those homes where men already
Are in wrong with the rulers.

An old friend loses his position,
Then his wife her trinkets —
Nothing fails like failure!

One lesson learnt from politics:
That he who once is wrong
Is likely to be wrong thereafter.
No matter where power passes
The gaols contain the same old faces.

Wrong of that woman to marry her spouse,
Wrong to stand by him,
Wrong to have things like rings in the house!
Right, right to be robbed!

Our burglars follow form,
Before they choose their victim
The press receives their scrutiny.
They follow in the footsteps of the law —
Oh jurisprudent citizenry!

Cats and Dogs

One has lived too long perhaps
In a country without cats,
Where the dogs strut by the fence
To keep far hence
The poor man, madman and the thief.

One has lived too long perhaps
In a land of cold-eyed cats,
Where no dogs go
With teeth and tail and tongue to show
Our woes are not unique.

Shabby Imperial Dreams

I confess with shame
That I have had such dreams.
My only plea is,
I was sleeping at the time —

The winding files of the military,
Who seem to be wearing Roman dress
(Not like this shapeless jungle army
In its carefully tailored rags),

The satraps and their curious recreations,
The consuls and proconsuls
(Not like these gentry in sober suiting
And shrewd but respectful expressions),

And myself, I admit,
A sort of Virgil in these proceedings,
Borne on a litter,
Dictating a letter,
Fed on the choicest local titbits
And the finest imported wines
— Spoilt, just a little,

With a slave girl,
Freed of course,
Set free by me,
To massage me
(Not like the thumbs and fingers
Of our noble Roman matrons),

And amicable natives, gaping gratefully
At an occasional hero hobbling past
(But no foot-rot or leech bites
Or the nausea contracted in the Naafi).

Who would not wish to be lightly looted
By such? What unnatural parent
Could grudge his daughter their attentions?
They speak in measured Latin,
With an English accent.
One of them looks like Enobarbus,
But more mature.
What stories he will have of the frontier!

— I wake to the morning paper,
And stories of expatriate officers
Discharged, sent home with compensation.
Another dream begins,
The dream of self-determination,
Self-empire.

One man's dream is soon
Another's nightmare.
Mine at least are posthumous,
Ruined castles in a vanished Spain.

Map

This is a map of the city,
Of the city's thoroughfares,
Where the big hotels are, and
American Express, and the banks,
The big shops and the temples.

This is a map of the city,
Of its thoroughfares, and the
Secondary streets, where the bars
Are, the small hotels and shops,
The blue films, and the massage parlours.

This is a map of the city,
Its thoroughfares, and its streets,
And the alleys, where the food stalls
Stand, and the city's women, and
Thin silver is beaten into bowls,
And wood carved into elephants.

This is a map of the city,
Its roads, and streets, and alleys,
The criss-crossed canals, and the
Hump-backed bridges over the canals,
Houses built high against flooding,
And the steep hauls up to the houses.

This is a map of the city,
In purple on brown, in relief,
On the ricksha-puller's legs.
Now that he knows his city,
Let him settle for a thoroughfare,

Where the big hotels are, and
American Express, and banks and shops,
A corner out of the sun, and
A begging bowl, at rest.

Big Feet

Bamboos round the door,
Banana leaves, still furled,
Ripe purple and erect.
Feet whispering on rushes,
Shadows, silks and silkiness.

What did we require? —
In tones not impolite, nor quite polite.
Sin was what we hoped for,
We did not know their word for sin.
Happily he seemed to see.

Though — no, alas —
With less than quite polite regret.
Perhaps the wrong place? he proposed.
Unless of course we brought it with us,
As for him, he had no licence,

No wherewithal for such.
(He pushed an ashtray over to us.)
It didn't tumble from the skies,
It didn't grow on trees.
A nice banana, then, a glass of tea?

Faults, yes, they had their faults,
For they were merely ignorant girls.
(Silks sighed, and bamboos railed.)
But was it sin to make mistakes?
A sin to be a simple girl?

Misunderstand they might, but
They could, yes, could understand;
A little rough, a little smooth.
For more than that — so he would say —
Better we should go back home.

Bamboos round the door,
Banana fronds about to bloom.
With dark tongues softly fretting,
Aggrieved silks hissing,
And our big feet retreating.

Processional

(for William Walsh)

Where are they all? —
The Chancellor and the Vice-Chancellor,
The Deputy Vice-Chancellor and the Registrar,
The Bursar, the Deans of the several Faculties,
The Director of Extra-Mural Studies,
The Estate Officer and the Librarian,
The Chairman of the University Council,
The Esquire Bedell and the Public Orator?

For the scaffolding has collapsed, the
Scaffolding of the impending Science Tower,
Has collapsed, with the long thin noise of the
Crumbling of a termite-riddled ivory tower.
And underneath are two female labourers,
Sought for by their colleagues like buried and
Perishable treasure. Now a trousered leg is
Uncovered, and pulled upon, and at its end is an
Ivory visage, a whitened stage concubine's,
Slashed with a vulgar wash of red.

And where is the University Health Physician?
(He is sick, he has left, he is on sick leave.)

And first will arrive the Fire Brigade,
With their hoses and helmets and hatchets
To exhume the already exhumed. And then
The police car with its mild unworried policemen
And hypnotic radio. And last of all,

In accordance with protocol, the ambulance,
To remove whatever the firemen and the policemen
Are no longer interested in.

But where are they all? —
The Development and the Public Relations Officer
And the various Assistant Registrars,
The Vice-Dean and the Sub-Dean of Law,
The Chairman of the Senior Common Room Committee,
The Acting Head of the School of Education,
The Readers and the Senior Lecturers
(The Professors we know are all at work),
And the Presidents respectively of the Local and
The Expatriate Academic Staff Associations?
This is a bad day for an accident.

Till a clerk arrives, a clerk from the
Administration, to administer the matter.
And order is imposed and sense is made.
The scaffolding consisted of old wood left out
Too long in the monsoon rains, and the women
Took too much sand up with them, because the
Contractor told them to get a move on, since he
Was hurrying to finish the job, because . . .
And they fell through four floors,
Carrying the scaffolding with them at each floor,
The sodden planking and the bamboo poles,
And now the scaffolding and the sand and the
Labourers all lie scattered on the ground.
The day and the hour are determined, and the
Victims identified as One Science Tower
(Uncompleted) and Two Labourers, Female, Chinese,

Aged about 20 and 40 respectively,
Who also look rather incomplete.

The Chancellor and the Vice-Chancellor,
The Deputy Vice-Chancellor and the Registrar . . .
There was little occasion for them after all.
The accident has been thoroughly administered —
Moved and seconded, carried and minuted.
A gaggle of idle Assistant Lecturers tap
On their watches, seditiously timing
The ambulance. And in the distance
The fire engine's bell can be heard already.

Poor Yusoff

Propped against the standpipe,
Yusoff contemplates his only friend,
A poem.
Standing there outside his race
(Which stands outside each other race),
At what remove from life
Does Yusoff stand?
He asks himself, that
Silent man, 'Am I
The saddest of the sad,
Or sad among the happiest?'
Saddled with religion,
Fraught with family,
And hobbled with linguistic cares.
There stands Yusoff,
Continence to one side,
Temperance on the other,
Indigence in the rear.
Poor Yusoff grumbles
(Thinking other people can)
'And I can't blame on riotous living
Verses uncompleted, crumpled sheets!'
Poor naked Yusoff
Props himself against the standpipe
(How would he rejoice
At water at his door?
He's no washerwoman).
His future all arranged,
Arranged in ruins,
Coldly sober there he stands, and

Contemplates his only friend,
A poem.
He must save his friend from ruin.
Yusoff turns the tap on.
Lo!
Words begin to flow.

The Mysterious Incident at
the Admiral's Party

Moored in his favourite Eastern port,
This jolly British Admiral
Must give a party on his ship,
With jolly guests, Malays, Chinese,
And Indians and English too.
Says he, 'I like the sarong well,
Trim gear, I wear it when I can.'
Good Jack, who likes Malay costume!
Approval flutters like the gulls,
Down go the drinks, up come the words.
'Although,' he says, 'it tends to slip,
It slips and slides below my hips,
It's hard to keep a sarong up.'
A Chinese lady speaks, sedate
And sweet. 'Then Admiral you need
A songkok.' Songkok as you know
Is headwear proper to sarong.
But Admiral and nearby guests,
They do not know what songkok is,
They think they hear some other words.
Some gape, some giggle and some gasp,
And jolly shaken Jack withdraws
Upon his bridge, and all disperse.
This Chinese lady at a loss,
She asks her spouse in Mandarin,
But what, but why? Who, unbeknown,
Now scouts about the huddled groups.
Then joins his wife. 'Ah me, my dear,'

He murmurs in their tongue, 'To keep
His sarong up — they thought you said —
The Admiral needs a strong — '
'For shame!' in spotless Mandarin
This well-bred lady cries, 'Oh filthy-
Minded foreign hounds! Oh deep disgrace!
What can they think of Chinese dames,
These British gentlemen? Away! '
So Admiral is hurt, Malays
Offended, English persons shocked,
And Chinese lady hates the lot.
Weigh anchor, jolly Admiral —
Let drop these oriental tricks,
Be stayed with buttons and gold braid!

Yours etc.

So many years
Spent hereabouts, spent
Well- or ill- , and
Only now I ask myself,
Not flippantly, sincerely
Ask myself: What
Does it mean? That
Meaningful word, that lexical
Phoenix, that Wholly of Holies —
Divine Sincerity?

I know that
Friends should be sincere,
Teachers should be sincere,
Writers should be sincere,
Politicians are not required to be,
Nor business men,
But grocers should be sincere.

(Why is it then my grocer proposes
To overcharge me a whole dollar
On a bottle of vermouth?
It is, he tells me sincerely,
A mistake, a sincere mistake.)

Sincerity means:
Not writing 'satirically'.
It means:
Not irony,
Which is the contrary of sincerity,

An altogether foreign devil.
(How can I believe what you say
When you say the opposite of
What you mean?)

It means:
Respecting the person who uses the word
With respect to you.
Or at least it means
A prompt and full apology
(Hand me my face back on a silver platter).
It means:
'No more Hiroshimas!'
It means (I begin to like this word):
A severe delimitation of literary criticism.

It is
(To confine oneself to its
Adjectival form, and this
Small jungly island where one sits in
Sincere cerebration)
The name of:
A Finance Company,
A Fertiliser Factory,
A Dispensary,
A Baggage Agency,
A Watch and Fountain Pen Dealers,
And something calling itself simply
Sincere Company
(What better company could a man wish for?).
It is also the name of a bar
Garnished with trim Chinese misses

(Sins Here?
Another Baggage Agency?).

Perhaps the secret is:
The word goes well into Chinese,
Into Japanese,
Into accents yet unknown,
As assimilable as beer,
Anti- whatever you disapprove of,
Pro- whatever you favour
(And if the worst should happen
Then your motives were sincere).
Verily a lamp unto thy feet!
Also, as the foregoing suggests,
Unamenable to dirty word play
(You will find few sins there).

Perhaps the secret is:
The word is a 1960's poem,
It sounds well and says little,
It causes no offence, it causes nothing.
All things considered,
The word is really a rather useful word

— Unless of course it is used
Sincerely.

The Tok-Tok Bird

The Tok-Tok Bird is in the tree,
Its clear and steady strokes
Beat out a neat reproach.
Whatever God may be,
He's not a novelist!
He has no mills at all but all he has is grist.

Whose rhythm is as pure as this?
Whose life so perfect in its plot?
Oh marble metrics of this bird,
Oh cool unfebrile song!
(The bird is also called Dong-Dong)
Oh long unblotted line with not one worried word!

Rueful Writers Contemplate a Painter

The Master, within a week,
Knocks off three paintings,
Well up to standard.

In his tiny studio,
Petrol and pandemonium outside,
And a minimum of view,

Irrespective of situations,
National pride and income,
This bloc and that.

How different from us!
Our stuff the stuff of politicians,
The cries of maddened cabbies

And spavined academics.
The whole day goes on washing words,
Scraping and scrubbing.

Within a week, the Master
Touches sweet oils to virgin canvas,
And makes three paintings.

To be hung,
To be chatted up,
And maybe bought.

Perhaps he even serves the State,
Even that perhaps —
Who can prove the contrary?

At least he does it no disservice,
As we contrive to do,
And sometimes do ourselves.

How shall we serve this Master —
Write notes for his new catalogue?
Old phrases waving grimy fists.

Unlawful Assembly

This vale of teargas,
More a hospital than an inn.

Clarity begins at home,
How far does it spread?

A gathering is a mob,
Mobs are to be dispersed

Back to their homes
(Lucky to have one)

Back to their jobs
(Lucky to have one)

Why subscribe to clarity?
In this vale of teargas

Should one enter a caveat,
Or a monastery?

After the Riots

The crickets are making throat-slitting noises.
I lie in the large darkness and cannot sleep.

Jumping with a fear which I am pleased to note
Is not entirely selfish, and sadness more than fear.

And true it is we live in tremulous times,
And the absence of a national consciousness.

Lying and thinking of friends, of a few friends,
Whose throats (who knows?) are being slit this moment.

We each bear all the rest some grudge or other,
Race, religion, colour, food, or even person.

So many grounds for so much throat-slitting,
For the noise of crickets, the noise of crickets.

The Minister desires us all to inter-marry,
Miscegenation is his measured policy.

The crickets are making kiss-kissing noises.
Vast checkerboard of wedlock, black on white.

Alack for Government! — Reduced to venery.
A national consciousness is born in bed.

The crickets sound like sawing wood for coffins.
They sound like someone sawing wood for bedsteads.

Love and death, such grand and soporific themes . . .
The crickets sound like someone making snoring noises.

Singapore

What mild magic
Hereto attaches? —

Rough draft or jotting
Jostling in my pocket.
Hot breast pocket, a
Tropic incubation? —

Maybe something there. Or
Will be. Where words may lead
Who knows? One, quite likely,
To another. Nile's crocodiles.

All day smell of durian,
Corpse-fruit in the streets.
Schools come out, Nile's flood
Of charms against oblivion.

Sunset simply shocking —
Artist's game or shame. Unless
You simply watch. And let
Hatch out what will.

At night last thing
A rustling in my shirt, tossed
To the laundry basket.
Cockroach — or dollar note?

No. Words blurred by sweat.
Yet, some mild magic.

Fact-finding

In the tropics,
Philosophies
Rot you like rain,
Far worse than whisky.

Who, by taking thought,
Shall keep the jungle back an inch?
Our thoughts go hand in hand
With cutlasses.

Are we afraid of Indonesia?
Does dragonish China haunt our dreams?
We contrive as best we can,
Today, as yesterday, why not tomorrow?
Circumstances change
And our contrivances change too.
We shall do as best we can —
That is our native talent.

And those who can't contrive
Can starve and almost starve,
Die and almost die,
Under whatever begging tongue,
Yesterday, today, tomorrow,
Under teeming Indonesia,
Under China's dragon tail,
As best they can.
That is their native talent.

'Aren't you afraid of Indonesia,
So few miles away?'

Our enemies were always close at hand.
You foreign friends alarm us more
With your huge questions,
Your mouth a foot away.
'Does dragonish China haunt your dreams?'
Not even your hard expectations
Haunt our dreams as yet.
We sleep deep at nights.

Poor in principles though we are,
Yet, there are spirits all about —
And one of them is human.
But in the tropics
Philosophies
Infect like standing water,
Rot far worse than whisky.
To us our tangled vegetation,
To you your tortuous theory.
Our gods are simpler,
They still want us to survive.

Go and Wash

Now go and wash yourself,
In a basin of poetry.
The water needn't be too clean,
Or one's hands feel shabby.

A question of degree,
And not shock treatment.
Shocks we have had in plenty,
Coolish cleanish water will do.

Water is transparent,
Water's the place for honesty.
You give and you take,
Exchange is no robbery.

One can smell of mortality
Too much, or too little. Perfumes
Of Arabia, songs of Araby,
Are not exactly what one wants.

Nor the recent antibiotics.
This stuff comes from the sea,
It's thicker than blood.
Now, hands, go and get dirty.

No Admittance

They will not follow you,
Not there. Not through that
Frosted-glass, sound-proofed
Self-closing door.

Behind a plastic-plated desk,
Flanked by phones and Olivettis,
You'll be safe! One tidy typist
Routs those uncombed ancient sibs,

Who know quite well
What projects see the light of day
In such aseptic cells,
What lustrous inside stories.

They will not follow you,
Not there. Anywhere but there.
Loth to discompose you,
You and your associates,

At your private labours.
As if it were publicity they chase,
Not you, and now prefer
To walk in noon-day's blaze.

Black markings on white papers,
Novels, verses, television scripts —
Anticipation makes their postures
Almost kindly,

Almost kindly
For a while, till they remember
That, even nowadays, where
Smoke is wanted, fire must be.

Meanwhile, perched on vinyl chairs,
The lank-haired ladies wait outside.
As you recount your errors,
Count your blessings too —

Orestes ran for years
To find a sheltering goddess.
You have your portable machine,
Or better still your typist.

They Who Take the Word

Playing with sorrows,
How unfit we are to face them
When real sorrows come —

Poetry unfits us,
Snowballs our small griefs,
And strips us

Where (like other creatures)
We need thick skins.
Yet maybe literature

Was meant like that:
Our own built-in defence,
Man's slight non-murderousness —

Meant to unfit us
For doing unsuitable things.
Our weakness was a strength.

But now no more.
Poetry's now an elective course,
Like Swahili, in the curriculum,

And nothing much outside.
Evolution had to write it off,
Affluence said the word.

Then what of us, the sad
And diffident monsters,
Stuck in primeval tear-stirred mud?

Maybe we can say:
And yet, it still defends us,
It unfits us

Now for loving life too much, too long.
It fits death in.
Weak can still make strong.

Back

Where is that sought-for place
Which grants a brief release
From locked impossibilities?
Impossible to say,
No signposts point the way.

Its very terrain vague
(What mountainside? What lake?)
It gives the senses nothing,
Nothing to carry back,
No souvenir, no photograph.

Towards its borders no train shrieks
(What meadowland? What creeks?)
And no plane howls towards its heart.
It is yourself you hear
(What parks? What gentle deer?).

Only desperation finds it,
Too desperate to blaze a trail.
It only lives by knowing lack.
The single sign that you were there
Is, you are back.

The Apple

That false knowledge you plucked
From the untrue tree
(What made you think it the true one?
Trees were born before you) —

That the flesh and the spirit
Are two.

Yet you made full use of your error
(Quite a fruitful apple!)
To suppose the deeds of the flesh are
Not precisely the deeds of the spirit

— Your ripest of alibis,
Compounded in tears and sighs,
In a wooden box in the church,
In a wooden box in the yard!

For in truth the two are one,
And this is the apple you missed,
This was the tree that you passed

(O happier fault,
In passing by, to find
A kindlier brand of guilt!)

For which is willing
— Can you tell? Or which is weak, or
Where exactly the scourge is falling?

In both you are blessed
Or in both you are cursed,
Your punishment pervasive,
Continuous your reward.

A few saints tasted the truth —
Extremists, or so you said,
Squalid, literal, uncouth,

But they knew
That sex is not something you have,
But sex has you.

For the spirit is made of flesh
(You saw its undoing made plain)
And the body is quick as the soul,
And their medicines are the same.

And this was what it meant
(That much reported event) —
The tree, the cross,
The apple you failed to pluck.
It had to be done all again,
It still must be done all again.

After the Dinner

After the dinner and its monstrous conversations
   — sex, murder and outrageous politics —
When your only contributions
Were dropping your glasses under the table and
    getting quietly fuddled,
Blind, dumb, blind —

But afterwards you triumph mildly
   — sex, murder and outrageous politics
All are forgotten. For they signify nothing
(Except to the reportedly raped or dead or deported),

While what you (spectacles *in situ,* and sobered
    by a sight of your host's bill) now write
Counts, or counts for a little.
Seeking in this slight and solitary act,
    in pen on paper,
To re-establish that in spite of everything
    (this evening's monstrous revelations)
The private life survives, and not quite everyone
    is murdered or raped, murderer or rapist.
That ordinariness has much to be said for it,
Is reasonably precious even, and precisely a matter
    for this extraordinary business of verse.

Alone in your beautiful bed,
In the new day's first hours,
In a storyless silence —
Almost you can hear the heavenly choirs,
You almost believe them.
    Nothing washes whiter than too much dirt.

Cultural Freedom

Set free
From all committee,
What would you write?

One writes despite,
In spite of failure,
Of failing light.

One works because
Of lack of leisure;
Out of loss

Of liberty;
To fill deficiency
With presentness.

You need defeat's sour
Fuel for poetry.
Its motive power
Is powerlessness.